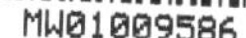

Angel of God, What's Your Name?

Angel of God, What's Your Name?

written by Rebecca McNall

illustrated by Joan Hutson

Nihil Obstat:
Very Rev. Timothy J. Shea, V.F.

Imprimatur:
†Bernard Cardinal Law
March 24, 1995

Library of Congress Cataloging-in-Publication Data

McNall, Rebecca.
Angel of God, what's your name? / written by Rebecca McNall ; illustrated by Joan Hutson.
p. cm.
Summary : Explains how God creates an angel to watch over and guide each person. Includes the "Angel of God" prayer.
ISBN 0-8198-0762-1
1. Guardian angels—Juvenile literature. [1. Guardian angels. 2. Angels. 3. Christian life.] I. Hutson, Joan ill. II. Title.
BT966.2.M28 1996
235'.3—dc20 95-30076
CIP
AC

Printed and published in the U.S.A. by Pauline Books & Media, 50 St. Paul's Avenue, Boston, MA 02130.

http://www.pauline.org e-mail: PBM_EDIT@INTERRAMP.COM

Pauline Books & Media is the publishing house of the Daughters of St. Paul, an international congregation of women religious serving the Church with the communications media.

Mighty Lord

Merciful Lord

Creator of all

Universal Love

Eternal Father

Divine Love

lmighty One

Heavenly King

Everybody knows God's name.
In fact, God has many names.

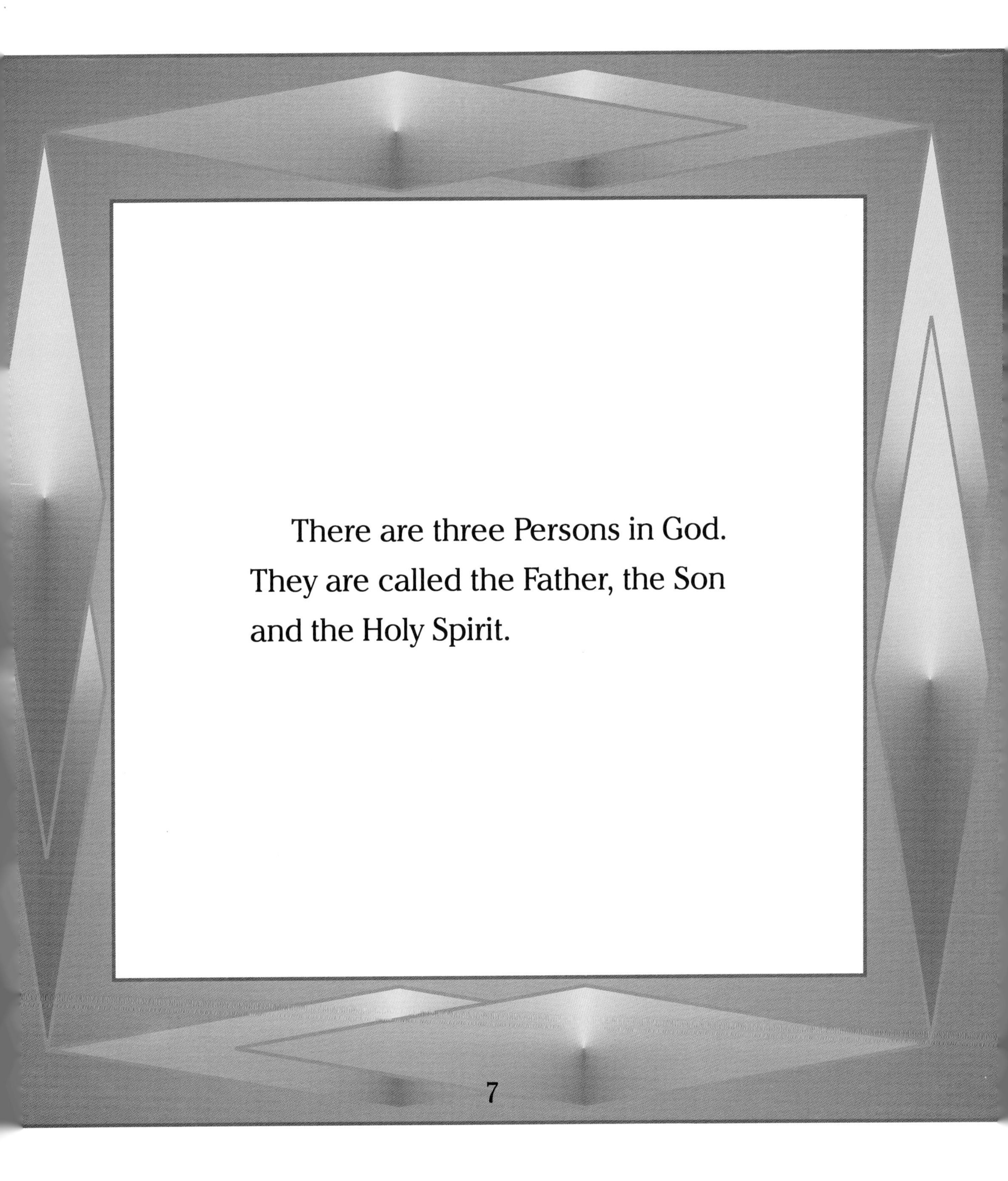

There are three Persons in God. They are called the Father, the Son and the Holy Spirit.

The Son is also called Jesus Christ.

Some people call God by the name Lord.
That's one of the names for God in the Bible.

We also know the name of the mother of Jesus. Her name is Mary, of course! She is known as the Blessed Virgin Mary.

Now, what about your guardian angel's name?

You don't know it,
do you?

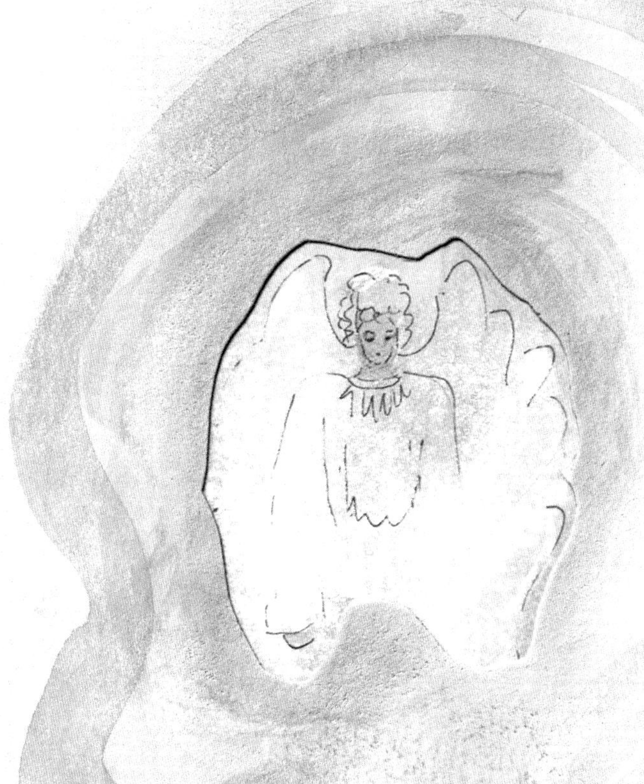

When you say the "Angel of God" prayer, can you picture your angel in your mind?

Have you ever thought about your angel?

God knows and loves your angel,

just like he knows and loves you.

Every angel is different.

God made each
one of them special

and gave each one
something special
to do.

Your angel is just for you!

Give your angel a name!

After all, he or she is with you

every minute of the night and day.

Your angel is praying for you, guarding you,

going with you everywhere you go,

even when you go places you shouldn't go.

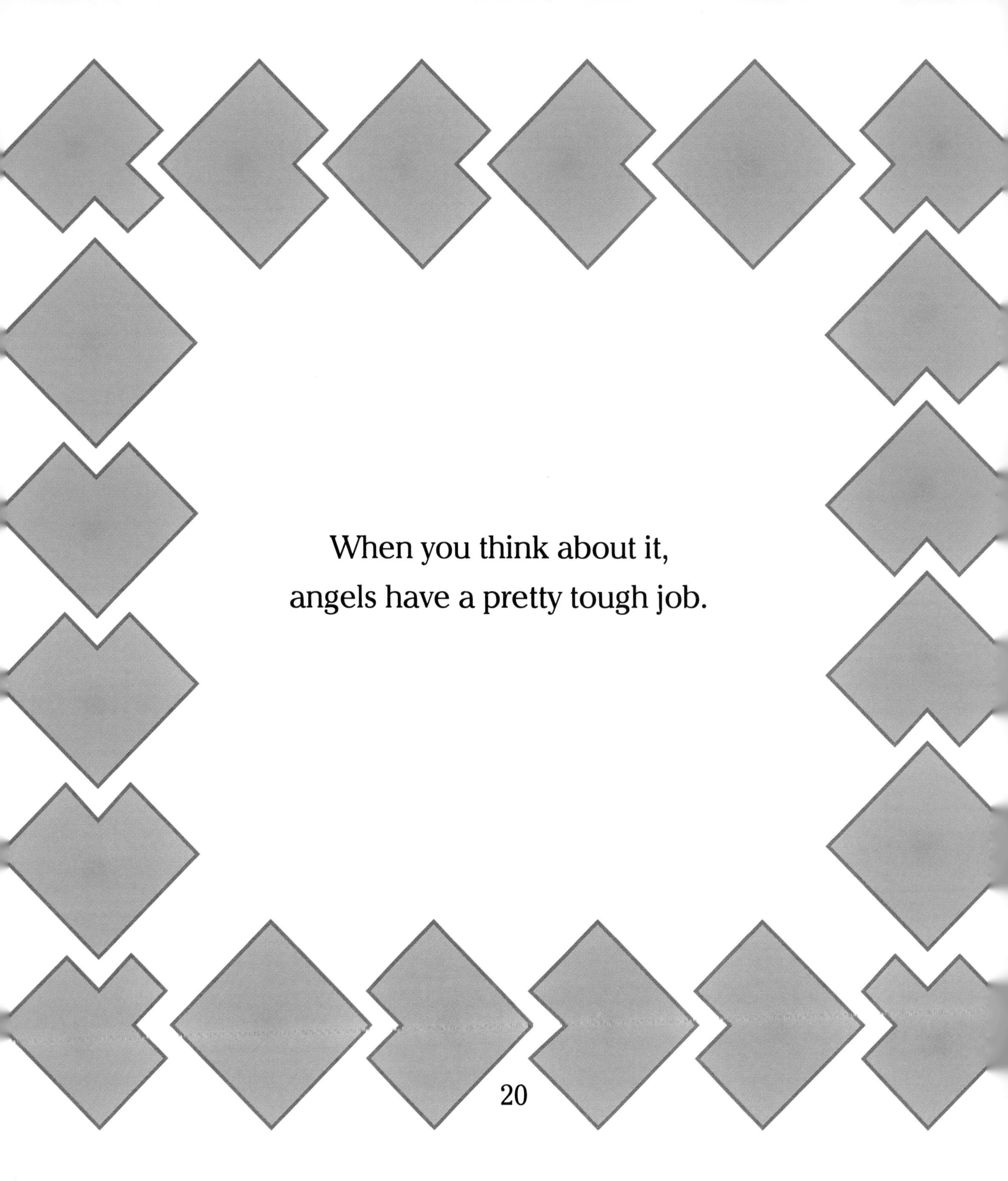

When you think about it,
angels have a pretty tough job.

They
sometimes
see things
they don't
want to see

and hear things they don't want to hear.

But they always stay right by our side and keep loving us and praying for us.

That's what God created them for.

God knew we'd need help in this world,

so he gave each one of us our own special angel!

My guardian angel is my best friend.

I named her Gloria.

What do you call yours?

Angel of God,
my Guardian dear,
to whom God's love
entrusts me here;
ever this day be at my side,
to light and guard,
to rule and guide.
Amen.

CALIFORNIA
3908 Sepulveda Blvd., Culver City, CA 90230   310-397-8676
5945 Balboa Ave., San Diego, CA 92111   619-565-9181
46 Geary Street, San Francisco, CA 94108   415-781-5180
FLORIDA
145 S.W. 107th Ave., Miami, FL 33174   305-559-6715
HAWAII
1143 Bishop Street, Honolulu, HI 96813   808-521-2731
ILLINOIS
172 North Michigan Ave., Chicago, IL 60601   312-346-4228
LOUISIANA
4403 Veterans Memorial Blvd., Metairie, LA 70006   504-887-7631
MASSACHUSETTS
50 St. Paul's Ave., Jamaica Plain, Boston, MA 02130
617-522-8911
Rte. 1, 885 Providence Hwy., Dedham, MA 02026   617-326-5385
MISSOURI
9804 Watson Rd., St. Louis, MO 63126   314-965-3512
NEW JERSEY
561 U.S. Route 1, Wick Plaza, Edison, NJ 08817   732-572-1200
NEW YORK
150 East 52nd Street, New York, NY 10022   212-754-1110
78 Fort Place, Staten Island, NY 10301   718-447-5071
OHIO
2105 Ontario Street (at Prospect Ave.), Cleveland, OH 44115
610-621-9427
PENNSYLVANIA
9171-A Roosevelt Blvd., Philadelphia, PA 19114   215-676-9494
SOUTH CAROLINA
243 King Street, Charleston, SC 29401   803-577-0175
TENNESSEE
4811 Poplar Ave., Memphis, TN 38117   901-761-2987
TEXAS
114 Main Plaza, San Antonio, TX 78205   210-224-8101
VIRGINIA
1025 King Street, Alexandria, VA 22314   703-549-3806
CANADA
3022 Dufferin Street, Toronto, Ontario, Canada M6B 3T5
416-781-9131
1155 Yonge Street, Toronto, Ontario, Canada M4T 1W2;
416-934-3440